Allyn and Bacon

Quick Guide to the Internet *for* *Educators*

Joseph D. Rivard
Central Michigan University

Allyn and Bacon
Boston · London · Toronto · Sydney · Tokyo · Singapore

A Viacom Company
Needham Heights, Massachusetts 02194

Internet: www.abacon.com
America Online: keyword: College Online

ISBN 0-205-26552-9

Printed in the United States of America

10 9 8 7 6 5 4 3 2 1   00 99 98 97 96

About the Author

Joseph Rivard is an Associate Professor of Education at Central Michigan University, Mt. Pleasant, Michigan. He has lectured extensively on issues relating to technology and education. Dr. Rivard's expertise in this area has garnished international acclaim. Lecturing throughout England, Scotland, Sweden, Canada, and the United States, Dr. Rivard has compiled this manuscript in response to frequently raised questions about the Internet.

When he is not about his professional responsibilities, Dr. Rivard enjoys spending time with his family, his dog, and his garden. He gratefully dedicates this publication to his Mother and Father.

CONTENTS

The author acknowledges the following corporations, manufacturers, products, and registered trade marks:

APA Publication Manual
America On Line
Archie
Chameleon
CompuServe
Delphi
GEnie
ERIC
H Gopher
Macintosh
Mosaic
National Geographic
Netscape
Newsweek
Porsche
Prodigy
New YorkTimes
Telenet
TIME Magazine
Turbogopher
U.S. News
Usenet
Veronica
Windows
Winsock
WS Gopher

Part One: What is the Internet?

Background and History

The Internet is a vast global network of computers connected to each other. While it is not uncommon for many computers to be linked together in an office or school network, the Internet has become the ultimate network because of its size. The Internet is the largest collection of computers connected by high speed telephone lines that has ever been tied together. Because of the number of computers online, the Internet allows an individual user to access and share innumerable information or communication resources.

The Internet began originally as a computer network established by the Department of Defense in the 1960s. It was considered a useful tool in establishing fast and efficient military communication. By the 1970s many major universities and research institutions joined this communication network. They began to share information resources via this new electronic backbone. The ease and speed with which individuals were able to communicate led large numbers of additional organizations to join the network.

By the late 1980s, the popularity of the Internet exploded. Users enjoyed the opportunity to access a wide variety of computer services and information, much of which was free. The number of information resources became so large that by the early 1990s many ordinary citizens felt they could benefit directly from the resources on the Internet. As there were already a large number of home computers in existence, all a citizen needed to do to get online was to create a link from their computer to the Internet. Linking a home computer to the Internet can be done in any number of ways which will be described in detail shortly.

Understanding the World Wide Web

The World Wide Web is one area of the Internet that has become especially popular. The Web makes extensive use of what some would call multimedia. In other words, the information accessed from the Web includes not only printed matter, but pictures, graphics, and sound as well. Getting around on the Web is especially user friendly because information topics can be pursued by simply pointing and clicking on topical titles. The Web is essentially a service provider which allows users to obtain a variety of information held within the resources of any number of computers on the Internet. The important thing to remember is that as the Internet grows, so to does the Web. Both constantly expand - much like gigantic spider webs alive with activity.

Web Organization and Content

Popularity of the World Wide Web is a result of its ability to make the diverse parts of the Internet more convenient to the user. The evolution of the Web has made access to the Internet much easier to both describe and use.

The Web is organized efficiently into three essential parts.

1. *Content:* The Web provides the user with a huge stockpile of information to read, view, or hear. Content within the Web is usually considered the most important of its components. After all, it is the information online that prompts most people to participate on the Internet, right? One might think of the Web as an electronic library of sorts. The Web has an ever-expanding array of topics. Some of the topics are very specific while others {such as "Education"}, are encyclopedic in nature. Information gleaned from the Web may take the form of printed matter, pictures or illustrations, sound, music, animation, and video.

In addition to the impressive assortment of reference information, the Web has become host to a great deal of commercial advertising as well. Much as our highway system has been marked with billboards advertising a variety of goods and services, our information highway is characterized in a similar fashion. The ads take the form of **Web pages** which companies create in order to provide consumers with product literature or catalog information. Some of these ads not only inform the user of product information, but allow the consumer to use the company's Web Page to purchase products while still online. Likewise, companies have created Web pages to provide consumers with product support after purchase. For example, access the Allyn & Bacon Web Page at http://www.abacon.com . These product support Web pages help decrease the load carried by 1-800 product support telephone lines. Web product support pages are sometimes less time consuming to use than telephone services plagued with voice recorded options and while-you-wait elevator music.

2. *Client Software:* Your computer needs software in order to get

all the information that is available on the Web. A Web *client* is a software program that lets you browse the content within the Web. Popular Web clients are **Mosaic** and **Netscape**. Much more will be said about these programs in Part Two of this Guide.

3. *Servers:* Much like the old adage which suggests no man is an island, the same applies to a computer on the Internet. In order to get all the good "stuff" on the Internet, you need to have access to all the other computers online. Severs are computers you can go to in order to get the information for your client software. An Internet server makes information available to online users. In order to provide the information to anyone who may request it, all the computers need to speak and understand the same *protocols.* In other words, they need to communicate in the same language. The business of computer protocols has become a bit sticky these days. There are so many different protocols it is difficult to keep track of them all. As a user, it really isn't necessary for you to understand all the technical stuff that accompanies computer protocols. However, there are a few basic vocabulary terms that you might find useful as you begin your journey on the information highway.

Tech Talk

Your First Internet Word Bank!

Browser: Software used for exploring the World Wide Web.

HTML: **Hypertext Markup Language**. Because of the diverse types of computers and computer software programs in use on the Internet there is a need to standardize the language protocols. HTML is the standardized language used on the Internet.

Hypertext & HTTP: **Hypertext Transport Protocol**. Hypertext is a type of document that allows convenient links to other documents. It is a very simple way of cross-referencing certain words, phrases, or symbols with additional information. Words or symbols that appear in color may be identified as *hypertext*. By clicking your mouse on these color coded words or symbols you are immediately linked to documents related to that field. The link may take you to another spot within a specific document, or it may link you to another site on the Web that contains related material to your source. HTTP is the protocol used for passing hypertext documents on the Web. Accessing the Allyn

& Bacon Web site will allow you to experience hypertext first hand. The address is http://www.abacon.com .

Mosaic: a software system that acts as a browser for the World Wide Web.

Netiquette: The use of appropriate communication on the Internet.

Netscape: a software system that acts as a browser for the World Wide Web.

Spiders: software programs that roam the Web collecting information for indexes.

Winsock: a standard that Microsoft Windows programs use to interact with the Internet.

URL: Uniform Resource Locator. High tech talk to arrive at a specific location. An Internet address.

NOTES

Part Two: Getting Started on the Internet

In order to get online, it should go without saying that you will need a computer. I recommend a computer with at least 8 mb RAM, although 4 mb can get the job done. The more RAM you have, the easier and faster you can work with and process information being retrieved from the Internet. It doesn't matter if you are using a Macintosh or PC Windows system, as long as a modem is connected to your computer. Some computers have built in modems; others do not. If you do not have a built in modem, you will need to purchase one. ***Modem*** is short for modulate/demodulate. This is the device which allows your computer to speak to other computers via a telephone line. The modem will dial up the required access number and put you online.

If you must purchase a modem, keep in mind that not all modems are created equal. Some move data more quickly than others. The faster your modem, the faster you can send and receive data and the less time your computer spends on the telephone line. Modem speed is described in **bps**, or *bits per second* sometimes referred to as ***baud***. Older modems transmitted at 1200 baud. Newer modems may transmit anywhere between 2400-9600 baud.

Once you have your modem and have properly connected it to your computer, be certain to plug the phone line into the modem before dialing up!

Internet Service Providers

In order to begin your journey on the Internet, you will first have to establish an *Internet Account*. This can be done in several ways. If you are a university student, you should be able to establish an account through the university computer services department. Your link to the Internet will probably be routed through the university mainframe, or some form of direct connection. The good news here is that your account may be free! The bad news is that an overloaded mainframe on your campus may result in not being able to log on whenever you want to. Daytime hours may be flooded with mainframe users, and you might not gain access privileges until evening hours.

Many individuals who do not have access to free university accounts may choose between either an *Internet Service Provider (ISP), or a Commercial Service Provider (CSP)*.

ISPs: There are a number of Internet Service Providers which are reasonable in cost. However many ISP's are dial-up bulletin board services, and may restrict the type of information you may have access to. Be careful of "bargain basement" dial ups, as they may have more accounts than can be easily handled. If you are a night owl and don't mind dialing up at 2:00 a.m., this might not be a problem. However, if you need consistent and spontaneous access to the Internet, question your ISP before writing a check. Ask them about the number of accounts they have in comparison to the number of telephone lines they control. Inquire about the <u>kind</u> of accounts they offer. Some dial up services only provide Internet E-mail services. This is a neat service for electronic correspondence and social chit-chat, but it is only one very restrictive use for the Internet. Consider also what your account will cost per month, how much online time you get for that fee, if the service provides news groups, if they have a customer support line, and if you need to install special software for your computer.

CSPs: Commercial Service Providers are an excellent way to gain access to the Internet if you can afford the monthly premiums. CSPs offer a large number of access plans, and do not restrict privileges to one type of information service. I have described several CSPs below.

<u>AMERICA ONLINE</u> - America Online was established in 1989 and has become a big hit with the general citizenry of our fair land. For the moment it is hailed as the largest online service, but there are many contenders for that crown. Part of what has contributed to AOL's popularity is the neat and clean interface that has been developed for the consumer. Upon subscribing, members are shipped a very user friendly graphical user interface {**GUI** - software to load onto your computer that will help you surf the Net}. The GUI is visually appealing and has numerous clickable buttons that give the user easy access to a host of consumer services that America Online can provide for their customers. AOL services include:

-- e-mail capability	-- file transfer	-- news groups
-- gopher interface	-- mail lists	-- online magazines
-- message boards	-- online tutorials	

America Online is unique in that is supports a single fee structure. In other words you pay a flat rate and have access to all AOL services. If you were a typical user who was online a few hours daily per week, your monthly bill would probably be around $50.00.

COMPUSERVE - The Compuserve Information Service {CIS} dates back to 1979 and was the first online Internet service. At that time CIS primarily served business interests and was primarily a text- only information source.

Compuserve was the first service to provide consumers with international access. In other words, it pioneered intercontinental e-mail service so that it made little difference if you were logging on from Michigan or the Middle East.

CIS provides its subscribers with a GUI {software to load onto your computer that will help you surf the Net} that is very flexible, but sometimes puzzling to the beginner. It features a BOW interface which is an acronym for "bunches of windows". For the experienced user it is pretty nifty to be able to open innumerable windows to navigate and explore from. For the novice it can be pretty scary and they may soon be lost in a maze of windows.

Other consumer criticisms for the CIS system have had to do with member addresses. Most online services allow you to select your own access name. Compuserve will assign you an account number as an ID source. This may be very efficient, but it removes some of the fun and personality of online identity.

News groups on CIS have traditionally focused on news and financial information. User demand has broadened the news group focus however, and Compuserve now features a healthy array of educational materials. The "Education Forum" has been an especially popular Compuserve feature. This service allows educators to do online projects together, download vast amounts of educational free-ware and shareware materials, or simply exchange ideas and opinions on diverse topics related to the field of education.

While Compuserve does have a lot to offer the subscriber, much of what is there is tricky to find. The bunches of windows make topical finds elusive, and the novice is better to seek and find through the use of "go" commands or search features at first. A nifty plus for each subscriber is the free subscriber magazine which will inform you of new service options and helpful tips for CIS consumers.

Compuserve has a much different fee structure than America Online. Subscribers pay a low monthly premium of about $10.00 . The trick here is that in order to get some of the really good materials that are online, you have to pay additional charges. This notion of Plus service charges is similar to premium channels on cable TV. Be wary if you are surfing and wander into the realm of a plus service! Compuserve's vigilant billing computers kick in and you could be surprised at how quickly your monthly charges can escalate. If you are not resistant to spontaneous temptations, you're better off to ask Compuserve for special navigator software. This software requires you to identify what areas of the Internet you want to explore before logging on.

PRODIGY A relative new-comer to the field, Prodigy was conceived in 1990. IBM and Sears were the proud parents of this new cyber child, and Mom and Dad hoped their child might help other children. Yup, an online service with a family focus! Prodigy features a multitude of topics, games, and news groups that are specially designed for families. Educational content is in high demand, and Prodigy even provides a special Classroom Prodigy service that is commercial free.

Prodigy is especially easy to navigate from, featuring large buttons to click on which lead subscribers to various screens with lots of options. Prodigy separates the "home, family, and kids" features from the "education" features by creating two separate button fields. The education button is located as a subfield within the area of "home, family, and kids". The reference and educational sources that are provided are immense.

Prodigy's fee structure is similar to Compuserve and Prodigy charges for what it considers extra services. On the down side, e-mail is considered an extra!

DELPHI - Delphi offers complete Internet access, but is not especially aesthetic. The interface is text-only, although it is fairly easy to navigate if you can remember all your control commands! No point and clicking here.

Delphi has a number of online shopping connections which is very appealing to some consumers. Subscribers won't need any extravagant software to load on start up. Just dial up and you're on your way.

Delphi offers two membership plans. The 10/4 plan gives you ten hours online for $4.00. The 20/20 plan gives you twenty hours online for $20.00.

GEnie - GEnie is noted for it multiple player games. The graphics developed by this service provider are tremendous! If you are looking for this type of entertainment, GEnie is for you. In addition to games, GEnie also provides news groups which have been divided into twenty-one categories. The "directory of roundtables" is what GEnie likes to call their discussion menu. While there is a lot here, it can be difficult to find. The effort may be worth it however, as GEnie does not charge extra for access to the categories within the Roundtables.

Evaluating the Best Service Provider

Before subscribing to any service that will take your hard-earned cash, it is best to consider what you really want from a service provider. Below are listed many of the more frequently used categories offered by Internet service providers. Which of these are most appealing to you? Check those that are of a *high priority for you.* By reviewing your needs and interests, choosing an Internet service provider becomes a bit easier.

Which services do you consider a priority?

Downloading files	____
Easy interface	____
Educational Topics	____
E-mail (free or toll)	____
Encyclopedia	____
Financial Info	____
Games	____
Help (online or toll)	____
Internet Access	____
Kids Stuff	____
Live chit chat	____
Magazines	____
Message Boards	____
Newspapers	____
News groups	____
Research	____
Shopping	____
Sports	____
Weather	____
Web Access	____

Keep in mind that a service provider such as Compuserve or America Online can give you access to the Internet. In and of themselves they are not the Internet. If you think of the Internet as a great highway, service providers are like gateways or "on ramps". Likewise, university mainframes or university direct-connection services are also gateways or on ramps. Each service removes many of the difficulties and challenges that one might face trying to go online without a service provider.

Service providers make using areas of the Internet easier through selective use of assorted software programs. Because the World Wide Web has become an extremely popular part of the Internet, developing Web client software has become big business. Prodigy has developed its own Web client. Other gateways use one of several well liked web clients. Two very popular Web clients are described below. It is very likely that regardless of your Net connection, if you navigate the Web you may end up utilizing one of the packages described here.

Web Client Software

NETSCAPE - Netscape has become the premier Web browser to date for several reasons. First there is the visual and aesthetic appeal. The graphics on Netscape are very well done. Furthermore, the graphic capabilities for those who desire to create Web pages are are very versatile. This versatility allows a Web user to manipulate not only text, but a mixture of textual and graphic information combined.

Netscape Basics

Information presented on Netscape appears in *hypertext*. A hypertext document allows many related topical themes to be connected by establishing *links*. Two frequently used terms in the world of hypertext are *link and node*. Links are those connections between the conceptual elements of a project, while nodes contain text, images, or other related information within your information base. A link is essentially a navigation pathway, while a node incorporates any of your content elements, be they text, images, sound bytes, or documents. The key to effective association in hypermedia are the ways in which nodes and links are related. The associations must be logical and make sense to users.

In Netscape links appear as underlined text. Using your computer mouse, place the pointer over any of the underlined text and click. Immediately you will be taken to a different document on the

Web.

Netscape always allows you to see exactly where you are {what your Web address is - i.e. the URL} by looking in the location indicator located near the top of the Netscape window. If you clicked on a link and decided that the document wasn't worth the journey, Netscape allows you to easily return to where you were by simply clicking the *back* icon in the tool bar or opening the *go* menu and selecting *back.* While this sounds simple enough, if you wander long and far enough, it is possible for a new user to get a little lost. Netscape provides an easy way for you to return *home* {to the very first page you started on}, by simply clicking on the *home* icon on the toolbar.

Keeping in mind that the Web can connect you to innumerable databases, you should realize that some documents will be much larger than others. The longer the document the more time it will take for the file you've clicked on to appear. The speed with which the document appears may also be a reflection of the modem you may be using or how many users are online. You will remember from Part I our discussion of modem speed and the implications speed has in relation to downloading files. If you selected a file that seems to be taking forever to download, Netscape allows you to cancel the selection by clicking the *stop* icon on the toolbar.

Many times you may already have a Web address that you found in a newspaper or magazine article. In order to get to that address you must tell Netscape where you want to go. One way that this can be accomplished is to select the File menu and choose the *open location* command. A location *dialog box* will appear. You must type the URL in the text box.

Please note! Typing in a URL must be done very carefully. Most Web addresses are rather long, lengthy, tedious to type, and it is very easy to mistype an address. Once you are certain that the address you have entered is correct, simply click the *open* button and Netscape will seek and find the document you desire.

Before ending our overview of Netscape basics you should realize that you can save files discovered on the Web to your own computer system (hard drive or disk drive). Saving files allows you to take documents with you for use in another location without requiring access to to Web. To save a file go to the File menu and select *save as.* You will be greeted with two options before the file is saved. You may save the document as a *source* document or a *text* document. By selecting *source* you will save all the appropriate formatting.

MOSAIC - Prior to the arrival of Netscape, Mosaic was the Web browser preferred over and above other clients. Mosaic was on the scene earlier than Netscape and pioneered the appealing graphical characteristics we have come to know and admire when navigating the Web. If you are unable to have Netscape at your command, Mosaic is the next best thing to have.

Mosaic Basics

Mosaic allows the navigator to accomplish the same fundamental operations described for Netscape. The user will need to take a little time to discern the subtle differences in the way Mosaic's toolbar is laid out however. Netscape users might criticize Mosaic's toolbar as less intuitive and thus less user friendly. There is a bank of tiny icons designed to do all the right things if you can figure out what all the symbols on the icons really mean. For example, the icon depicting an open folder launches the dialog box for entering a URL. The floppy disc icon is supposed to suggest a save to disc feature, while arrow keys imply forward and backward movement through document addresses. The home key is adequately characterized as a little house, and the print key aptly features a printer icon. Good luck interpreting the code for Mosaic's find, paste, and copy clipboard icons!

If you become irritated with the Mosaic toolbar you can always eliminate it all together by hiding it (open the *options* menu and click on *show toolbar*). Once removed you might more successfully navigate through the use of conventional menus placed atop the computer screen.

Navigating Naturally

Early on I stated that for the most part it makes little difference if you are a Macintosh or PC Windows user. I reiterate that notion once again, but let me take a moment to qualify some of the idiosyncrasies of using either system. Below I have listed several things that Mac and PC Window users should be aware of when subscribing to an Internet provider, navigating the Internet, or browsing the Web.

1. Internet providers will usually provide you with all the right software tools upon establishing an account. *You will need to indicate* when you establish your account whether or not you are a Mac or a PC Windows user. Net tools that are provided for either platform typically include:

- ◆ E-mail - so than you can send and receive electronic mail
- ◆ Gopher - to locate information on the Internet
- ◆ Veronica - a search tool
- ◆ FTP - a device for retrieving files on the Net
- ◆ Archie - a locating tool
- ◆ IRC - a tool that allows "live chat" in the Net
- ◆ Usenet - a search and read tool to access discussion topics
- ◆ Web client - software to explore the World Wide Web
- ◆ Telnet - a terminal on remote computers

2. Not all commercial service providers have Web access, and those that do may have constraints. For example, Prodigy has a Web browser that works great for PC Windows, while Mac users are left out. This will be remedied soon.

3. GEnie's front end GUI is only available for PC Windows.

4. A small and sometimes unnoticed ISP known as eWorld was available only to Mac users at first. It is just now exploring the PC Windows market.

5. The *save as* option in Mosaic works simply for Mac users while PC Window users were unable to have required to have the opportunity to save a file as straight text or in HTML format. This has been rectified in current versions.

NOTES

Part Three: What The Internet Can Do For You

The reasons for going online are as diverse as the people who log on. Business organizations and research institutions avail themselves of the tremendous communication and information resources that the Internet provides. Many families appreciate not only the information resources but the entertainment and online shopping features as well. Students enjoy abstract materials, the unending access to reference databases, as well as the opportunity to communication socially and academically across the miles. Below are listed a few of the most typical kinds of things available on the Internet.

❑ E-mail - Electronic mail allows you to have an address on the information highway. Within an instant you can send or receive messages to any number of the +30 million Internet users around the globe. E-mail can be sent or received despite the Internet service provider to which you are connected. A Compuserve user can just as easily communicate with a university mainframe user, a direct connect user, a BBS user, or an America Online user!

❑ Newsgroups - Newsgroups are essentially message boards. People read messages related to a myriad of subjects and are able to post messages about other people's messages on the Internet. It's kind of an international public forum - a large scale, electronic town meeting. Everyone can have their say on any given topic and receive feedback on individual thoughts, opinions, and suggestions.

❑ Usenet - Usenet consists of a very large collection of newsgroups. Some are very academic and scholarly, others may be amusing and fun, while still others may be adult-oriented and sexually explicit. Users should keep in mind that the Internet is not monitored or policed. Some types of language and/or content expressed in some newsgroups may be considered offensive by some individuals.

❑ Mailing Lists - These lists are essentially the same as any newsgroup, however messages are not posted generically. Messages are sent directly to your e-mail address.

❑ Web Sites - Visiting the Web gives users a break from text only Net surfing. You can experience refreshing multimedia based information. Information gleaned from various Web sites may contain pictures, graphics, animation, sound, or video information.

❑ BBS Service - Accessing a Bulletin Board Service entitles you to any/all of the information posted on the select theme of the BBS. The BBS theme is generally established by the SYSOP or *systems operator.* A Sysop might be a university professor or a teen-age hacker with a passion for mountain bikes. One element that has made the BBS service so alluring is the notion of *live chat.* Live chat is a form of e-mail, however you are simultaneously exchanging text based conversation person-to-person. Live chat lines might be established for academic purposes, entertainment purposes, or social purposes. Keep in mind that live chat is not policed or monitored, and individuals should be wary of divulging personal information online. Both children and adults should be warned of the dangers of live chat, as some criminal elements have met their victims as a result of live chat Internet introductions.

Internet Precautions

Keep in mind that in the world of cyberspace users have a great deal of anonymity. Many find great security in the fact that they are able to communicate with a host of individuals without ever having to provide them with personal information. Most Netters are identified with quirky code names or ID numbers.

While such anonymity can work for you, there are risks that every Netter needs to be aware of. Once online, it is very difficult to know exactly with whom you are communicating. People can take on any number of false identities, or pretend to be any number of personalities. Much of this is done in a harmless social context. Some of this is done with criminal intent. The bottom line is simply this:

- ⇨ never release your first and last name
- ⇨ never divulge your resident address
- ⇨ never publish your home phone number
- ⇨ avoid making reference to where you work or study
- ⇨ never reveal account passwords
- ⇨ never forward a pict file (picture) of yourself

Realize that many commercial service providers will ask you to fill in a *member profile* upon subscribing. There is nothing wrong with listing the type of hardware you use and your interests and hobbies, but be careful to avoid supplying personal data. Some individuals even prefer keeping their gender anonymous. This is easily done by selecting a code word that suggests neither gender.

Regardless of your precautions, individuals can still become the target of unwanted Internet communications. These communications may be intimidating, threatening, or found to be offensive by the receiver in any number of ways. Early in your Internet experience be certain to learn how to *log* online chat, e-mail, or messages. By compiling an accurate log of these communications you will be able to submit evidence to your Internet service provider. With your documentation there is a better chance that the service provider will be able to track the offender and have the individual purged from the system.

Netiquette

What is proper and what is improper communication on the Internet? A part of this issue lends itself to discussion of freedom of speech and expression, as well as academic and intellectual freedom. Few have endorsed the notion of censoring the Internet, simply because trying to discern what is universally offensive seems to be an impossibility. Some pict files (pictures/photos) might be considered entertaining or artistic by some and pornographic by others. Assorted words are considered obscene by some, crude by others, and unexceptional by still others.

At present, the boundaries for these types of issues are relatively undefined. Some commercial service providers have made recent strides to monitor the sending and receiving of assorted pict files. Materials deemed pornographic in nature have resulted in the procurement of criminal charges against various sender/receivers. Likewise, many CSPs will remove you from the system if in your communication you are prone to using inappropriate language. CSP violations typically consist of a thirty day suspension for whatever is considered a violation of service terms. The extent to which these types of penalties increase or decrease are likely to reflect both consumer expectation and political caucus.

Netiquette considers far less serious and foreboding issues as well. Remaining attentive to some of the following rules will help you surf the Net without getting your feelings hurt.

1. Tangents - Experienced netters really get upset if you join a discussion group without taking the time to get acquainted with the topic and the issues. Tangents are a big pet peeve, so try to stay focused and communicate with both a point and a purpose.

2. Never type in ALL CAPS. Netters interpret this as being yelled at!

3. Learn a few simple Netiquette symbols:

:-) = a smile
;-) = a wink
:-(= sadness
:-D = laughter
<g> = grin
<vbg> = very big grin
:-* = kiss
%-) = confused
:-| = boring

4. Netiquette shorthand - Once online, there are a number of ways to communicate well, and reduce the number of keystrokes one might type in order to send a message. You might like to learn a few of the more popular short strokes.

ADN = any day now
B4N = bye for now
BBL = be back latter
BTW = by the way
CU = see you
{Chris} = hug to Chris
{{{Chris}}} = lots of hugs
IC = I see
ILY = I love you
IMO = in my opinion
J/K = just kidding
OIC = Oh, I see

5. Flame broiled or fried? Just about the time you are really starting to enjoy surfing the net, chatting online, sending and receiving e-mail, you will probably get *flamed*. Getting flamed is a Netter's term used by some in reference to receiving rude, nasty, or meticulously

critical communications. There are those on the Net that especially enjoy flaming newcomers online. These individuals will go to great lengths to insult you because of your online inexperience or lack of Net vernacular.

There are additional situations that may set you up for getting flamed. You might be responding to a bulletin board message or sharing in an online debate or discussion group. Inevitably there will be someone who disagrees with your opinion. Instead of trying to argue a point with intellectual reason, some individuals will try to intimidate you with scathing criticisms about your character or writing style.

Of course there are the subtle, sneaky, humorous flames that may occasionally pop into your e-mail slot as well. These flames start out very cordial - even down right friendly! Gradually the communique begins to weave in arrogant and critical commentary against you. By the time you are finished reading the note there is little doubt in your mind that you've been had. The fiery reach of the Internet flamer knows few limits. Keep in mind that there is a difference between getting flamed and being harassed or threatened. Personal threats or harassments should be logged and reported to your Internet Service Provider.

For some, flaming has gotten to be a game. They consider it a part of the Net entertainment venue. Others become very upset by the hostility present in such correspondence. For those of you budding flamers, I encourage you to fine tune your flaming skills on Internet newsgroups dedicated to such verbal battery. For example, Usenet features a "Hall of Flame" {alt.flame.hall-of-flame}. By localizing your attacks to other like-minded people, you'll allow the rest of the Internet population a well deserved sigh of relief.

NOTES

Part Four: Educational Applications of the Internet

Let us Wax Philosophic...

Today's teacher has at their disposal more educational tools than ever before. When we think about new learning technologies and the ability to use the Internet as an information highway, we are wise to keep in mind one thing: they are tools. Technology has provided us with these additional tools to use in harmony with the many other tools that are at an educator's disposal. The tool in and of itself is only as good as the teacher who puts the tool to good use.

In order to make Internet technologies work effectively, it is prudent for teachers to understand the role of information and instruction in today's world. *Technological literacy* is a term which refers to the extent to which people are aware of the role technology plays in the distribution, acquisition, and synthesis of information. Upon entering the world of the Internet, teachers are immediately confronted with the vast information stores available. It is easy to ask yourself this question. Now that I have access to all this stuff, what do I do with it?

The mere quantity of information currently available is influencing learning is profound ways. Teachers must innovate creative ways to establish new relationships amidst knowledge bases. In this regard, the Internet can be very helpful in presenting to students real world examples of *integrated knowledge*. Knowledge on the Net is organized in numerous ways, but it is typically presented in a relational way, or in accordance to related fields. Web-constructed hypertext allows students to see the connections between knowledge fields, and allows them the opportunity to pursue knowledge not in a linear or chronological way (the way most books do), but in a relational way.

Much of the information on the Internet is also *real world knowledge*. It is knowledge related to human interests and endeavors. It is knowledge that continually expands with individual input. It is knowledge that is gradually constructed. It is knowledge which can be interacted with, manipulated, added to, or subtracted from. At its best it is a "living" body of knowledge.

Teachers who encourage their students to work cooperatively in small groups will find that the Internet really does promote *collaborative learning*. The mere fact that the Internet is so vast may encourage students to do team information searches. When returning to combine information sources, it is unlikely that any two students will have accessed the same material or will have summarized or interpreted the data in the same way. This will provoke great discussion. As your students condense all of the information in preparation for sharing a group presentation, they will be reminded that some information is more important than other information. Students will intuitively establish a type of knowledge scaffold, which will prioritize information gleaned from the Net.

As educators we must realize that we cannot efficiently teach all of the information that currently makes up the world's knowledge base. In fact, it is not only impossible, but imprudent to consider the collecting and depositing of knowledge as the essence of education. Teachers who utilize the Internet in their classrooms should not be controlled and overwhelmed by the information available. Quite the contrary. Teachers need to use the Internet as a vehicle which gives control over information. Internet technologies provide a means by which students are able to *construct* knowledge schemes through individual searches, group dialogues, and guided instruction. I often refer to this type of learning as *architectural learning*. Students online are equipped with the ability to interrelate and manipulate knowledge fields. They are offered opportunities to modify concepts in order to arrive at predetermined learning outcomes.

The Internet can really work to a teacher's advantage as both an instructional and professional tool. Teaching can become easier and more rewarding as we add this tool to our already diverse assortment of educational tools. Like tools employed in any other instructional method, good teachers will thoughtfully plan for its introduction to the students. An Internet excursion should provide students with experiences that develop skills, and encourage personal and academic growth. Teachers should avoid using this technological medium as a tool for free time entertainment or an inconsequential appendage to our curricular vision. It must become an integrated part of the educational process, enmeshed within the fabric of our curriculum.

Technology Based Lesson Plans

Every educational application of Internet technology should begin with a good lesson plan. Minimally, this will consist of:

- ✻ two or more broad instructional goals
- ✻ a defined set of learner outcomes
- ✻ a description of materials required

* an outline describing instructional methods and procedures
* a listing of student activities and responsibilities
* an instructional time line
* a comprehensive assessment plan that identifies the procedures for evaluating student performances.

Because your lesson plan is based on use of the Internet, the **broad goals** that you establish in your plan should focus upon one or more of the following *information handling skills*. The information age skills that you are broadly addressing include:

1. **Helping students "handle" large volumes of electronic information stores.** The ability to determine what information is needed before going online so as not to become "lost" in a sea of information sources.

2. **Developing skills which help students identify information that is essential and related to the task at hand.** Information identification skills also include developing proficiencies which aid students in prioritizing and scaffolding information schemes, helping students arrange information sources in increments of greater and lesser importance.

3. **Developing information acquisition skills.** After identifying relevant information, students must be competent in knowing how to acquire that information. In the least this should include an understanding of Web links and hypertext formats, printing hard copies of information, saving online files to disk, etc.

Learner outcomes should be more precise and serve as the culmination of specific performance objectives. Regardless of your topical plan {seeking information on Civil Rights, Insects, Weather, or Current Events...}, *information age skills* that you should specifically regard include:

1. *Information analysis* - the separating and dissecting of information so that it may be studied, examined, and analyzed.

2. *Information application* - the ability to apply the information found in a search activity and relate that information to the task at

hand. Putting the information to a purposeful use.

3. *Self evaluation skills* - encouraging students to consider the value of the information acquired. How well did all of the information sources "fit" together to complete a whole? How does the student feel upon task completion, what is their reaction to the product of the lesson? Self evaluation should include an examination of what went right and wrong within the learning process.

TBLPs and Assessment Issues

As teachers increase the number of technology facilitated learning opportunities for students, they must also address important *assessment issues.* Applying Internet lesson plans in your classroom will require you to consider carefully how the fruit of student labor will be appraised.

Lesson plans that make use of Internet technology will require teachers to spend more time assessing thought and the products of thinking as opposed to assessing right and wrong responses to a conventional quiz or test instrument. Your assessments must involve the evaluation of student choices, decision making skills, interpretive skills, analytical skills, and applied skills. The evaluation plan should define mechanisms for teacher evaluations of student competence and growth, *and* mechanisms that allow student self examination.

For years teachers have been struggling to facilitate learning that transcends the mere knowledge level of Bloom's taxonomy. Internet plans can help teachers facilitate knowledge which requires higher level thought. Assessing higher level thought requires a scheme different from those used in assessing lower level knowledge forms. One construct teachers have found especially adaptable to Internet lesson plans is the *performance based assessment system.*

Performance based assessments require learners to be submitted to a real world learning environment. The Internet fits that description nicely. It is a real world environment which will require students to perform in conditions that are filled with the interjections of other human and non-human information entities. Each exposure to a real world Internet experience requires the learner to perform in the midst of online interactions, commentary, discussion, and critique by a host of players.

It is common knowledge that teachers assess competence for two reasons. Frequent assessments contribute to increased learning and increased motivation. One might argue about how a quiz or test increases motivation, but it is evident that for many students they really do! Consider then, how much more a performance based assessment system could enhance learning and motivation. Much of what we do in the pursuit of daily living requires real world, "on the job" performances. In many respects it is knowing that our performance is depended on that encourages us to do quality work (Sizer, 1984). Knowing that our performances are evaluated by external authorities motivate an individual to perform well and increase their efficiency. This type of reasoning can be present in any real world learning scenario.

Let's consider for a moment what constitutes a student performance so that we can better envision what a performance based Internet plan might require.

➜ Performances require preparation: The learner must prepare, practice, experiment and self evaluate.

➜ Performances are created: Learners must share an interpretive point of view.

➜ Performances require performing: Learners are required to demonstrate competence before or amidst others.

➜ Performances are interactive: There is a give and take between a number of participants.

➜ Performances receive immediate feedback: Learners realize the impact of the actions in an immediate sense.

➜ Performances are social: Learners gain satisfaction and input from an audience via conversation, interaction, appreciation, praise, and criticism.

➜ Performances are judged: Others provide commentary on how to improve a performance.

➜ Performances are qualitative: Success is measured by "degrees of quality" in demonstration.

Performance based education is not really a new phenomena. In the past however, it has been relegated to educational venues that have not always been academic. As the number of academic fairs, science fairs, and academic olympic events increase, we begin to see how performance based assessments are beginning to catch on. Now that the Internet has arrived on scene, teachers are afforded one more way to implement a performance based learning opportunity.

Benefiting From Performance

The benefits of implementing performance based assessment are many.

- The quality of content related materials can be interpreted with greater accuracy. The product provides evidence of real world competency.

- The assessment is more holistic and comprehensive. Evaluations are not made from randomly sampled student responses.

- Students become part of the evaluation process and become self invested in their work.

- The assessment may be multidimensional as the work requires a number of higher level cognitive capabilities.

- The assessment may more accurately define student strengths and weaknesses

- The assessment rewards innovation, creativity, and individuality.

Improving Instruction with TBLPs

Technology based lesson plans which utilize Internet resources improve instruction in many ways.

1. **Students online are *actively involved*.** The are immersed in a system which requires attentiveness and interactivity. They are constantly making choices and decisions which result in immediate consequences. They are allowed to investigate information sources in a

trial and error manner. They are free to reverse their tracks and head out in new directions. They pursue knowledge actively and personally.

2. **Students online are able to see knowledge in *relational* ways.** Information links are established for students so that they are better able to construct knowledge based upon concepts that are connected together.

3. **Online experiences effectively merge higher level thinking and the application of basic skills.** Basic skills are necessary in order to read and identify information sources, however students are unable to make choices about information without engaging in higher order thinking skills.

4. **Students online have the opportunity to delve deeply into subjects and themes.** The immense nature of the Internet allow endless opportunities for students to explore with a limitless capacity. Teachers are relieved of the burden of providing students with source materials. Time spent collecting library samples or establishing reserve stacks may be quickly replaced with time spent with students as they return from the search experiences. Both the student and the teacher's rate of productivity can increase because students have an endless stream of easily accessible subject materials.

5. **Students are able to work both individually and in groups.** When working independently, learners are afforded the luxury of establishing their own working pace. When reporting collectively students benefit from sharing information and exchanging ideas and opinions.

Citing Information Sources

When utilizing information that is gleaned from the Internet, students and teachers should note that it is appropriate to cite Internet sources. Internet users should observe the same ethical considerations when manipulating Internet information as they would if they were using text based materials. Every effort should be made to reference source materials, credit graphic representations, and/or cite the databases from which information was retrieved. Users may choose from among any APA reference formats.

1. E-Mail

Author (date). Subject [e-mail to receiver's name], {Online}. Available e-mail: receiver's e-mail address.

2. Articles via mail lists

Jenkins, J. (1996). Everything You Ever Wanted to Know About Johnny. RJKE-FW3. Available e-mail: LISTSERV@cmu.ehhs.edu. Message: GETJON01=Mail.

3. Online database

The Jenkins Directory. [Online]. (1996). Available: Jenkins Index File: The Jenkins Directory (EDUA7).

REFERENCES

Sizer, T. (1984). Horace's Compromise. Boston: Houghton-Mifflin.

NOTES

Part Five: Online Learning

A Little Theory Goes a Long Way...

Teachers will find that the Internet is a tremendous tool for online learning both inside and outside of the four walls of a conventional classroom. Recent advances in Internet connectivity are nothing short of spectacular. Yet the super intelligent networks that are being created for government, business, industry, and education, will dwarf what may currently amaze us with even faster and more colossal networking capabilities.

Because the technological disposition of our society is changing and evolving so rapidly, it is imperative that today's educator work hard to keep abreast with the advances that can impact educational practice in positive ways. Few teachers have had time to immerse themselves in the technological revolution, so don't feel isolated if you feel rather intimidated by the imposing arrival of technology in your district. My best advice is to begin with small steps. Learn how to use the new tools at your disposal, and accept the reality that education must constantly change in both its physical and methodological constructs.

Internet technologies easily allow us to go beyond the four walls of our classrooms. We limit the many opportunities students have today if we perceive education as something that is only accomplished within conventional classroom settings {see the short story at the end of this chapter}. Today, the *world can be your classroom!* The variety of experiences available to students and teachers should provoke us to tap into the new resources in conjunction with our buildings, books, and bulletin boards.

Online learning requires each of us to keep in mind that information is structured quite differently than what we may be used to. Conventional instruction attempts to create linkages between prior knowledge which exists within a student's field of experience and new knowledge which may extend beyond a student's field of experience. The linkages are often created in step like fashion. They are also frequently linked in a chronological and conceptually sequential manner. Conventional teaching supplements {trade books, video, slides, etc.} are likewise contrived in rather linear ways. Teachers and students are comfortable with exposure to information that is presented in these types of expository or narrative formats.

Many online learning experiences expose us to information presented in radically different ways. The World Wide Web requires us to process information presented via multimedia and hypermedia formats. Multimedia has been defined as information presented in any given combination of text, graphic, animation, or video source, delivered via a computer host. *Hypermedia* combines multimedia with some form of program which allows for greater interactivity between the user, the software, and the hardware. Hypermedia allows audio and visual information to be linked together in ways that allow a user to navigate through layers of related information.

Because information in hypermedia is presented associatively {linking related concepts together} and not in linear or chronological ways, hypermedia seems especially conducive as a tool to facilitate learning in our students. Many have found that the creation of layered information stacks through hypermedia replicate the way in which concepts are formed in the human mind, linked together, built upon, and expanded - based upon prior knowledge and association.

Each student brings to the learning experience a highly individual domain of prior knowledge and experience. Learners draw different associations between new and former knowledge deposits. Hypermedia may become the ideal medium for both the delivery of new information *and* the synthesis and manipulation of previously acquired information. Hypermedia should not be recognized simply as an information conduit which mainlines information between a source and receiver. Rather, hypermedia might be considered an external pool of *schemata* or schemes. Schemes are considered internal mental structures by which individuals organize their environment. As learning occurs, knowledge schemes are modified or changed as information is identified, processed and stored. Hypermedia becomes an *external* pool of knowledge concepts through which learners are challenged to make new associations. External Internet information sources become audio and visual categories from which individuals can internally classify and store specific information and experiences.

Internet lesson plans can establish a *relationship* between external and internal schemes. The associations in the external pool are manipulated in much the same way knowledge associations are made within the internal cognitive structure of the learner. Learning with hypermedia is an exercise in *associative learning,* a fundamental principal of schema theory. It is consistent with what we know about the ways in which humans process and organize information.

Learning with hypermedia may be disorienting for adults only because adults have become accustomed to narrative and expository knowledge bases which are conceptually sequential and often linear.

Children have fewer years invested in the accumulation of linear knowledge and more readily invest themselves in opportunities with hypermedia. They have also become accustomed to the the structure of hypermedia presentation through many of their electronic entertainment games.

Hypermedia allows learners to interact with concrete audio, visual, pictorial, and graphic experiences. As they interact with new information they are allowed *control* over the manner in which information is linked, arranged, or ordered so that learners can most efficiently integrate prior knowledge experiences with new information. Hypermedia is especially effective for bridging concrete information and abstractions. Hypermedia also brings a certain realism to the lesson. Learners are often more receptive and willing to respond and perform the tasks before them.

With conventional instruction serious consideration must be given whenever teachers attempt to incorporate "real world" supplements to text based instruction. Going to a museum, watching a video, or interpreting abstractions with conventional instructional tools have to be planned in very precise ways. The time and planning required for each is often less than practical. Because most instructors find themselves short on time {and/or resources, transportation, etc.}, teachers find that the greatest amount of information can be presented in the least amount of time by using linear, sequential, and chronological printed or aural materials. This accounts for a preponderance of print delivered information and direct teaching activities. Issues of time management and limited resources usurp the implementation of many our best interpretations and applications of contemporary learning theory. However, Internet technologies in association with hypermedia now afford teachers and students real world experiences in ways that are personally attractive, meaningful, and practical.

Lesson Launchers

Part four of the Quick Guide detailed how to construct a well organized technology based lesson plan utilizing the Internet. What follows are just a few ideas to help you begin. After all, the best plans have to start with ideas! Keep in mind that I do not know the grade you are interested in teaching or what subject you might want to develop a plan for. These lesson launchers are simply notions to help you brainstorm. No one could ever compile an exhaustive list of the many different ways of using Internet technology in the classroom. Once you begin using the Internet yourself, you'll be able to come up with many more ideas. Undoubtedly you will then think *your* ideas are much better than mine!

Please note: Observe all the appropriate **cautions** discussed in part three of this Quick Guide!

❒ Career day: Gather information from adult users online. It's amazing to consider the host of professions represented!

❒ College prep: Get ready for those pesky admission exam requirements, gather information on colleges and universities your Seniors might like to attend, or read campus newspapers.

❒ Current events: Use any of the conventional newspaper activities that are available, but make the assignment an online effort instead of a paper and pen affair.

❒ Debates: initiate an online debate on a hot topic. Log the responses and content for distribution and class discussion.

❒ Environment: The Internet is filled with environmental forums which deal with many of the issues K-12 educators frequently tackle. Add a technological component to your environmental units. Search AOL with key word "EForum", Compuserve with "Go Earth", or Prodigy with "JUMP: Green Connection". Interesting Internet Gopher sites include "envirolink.org", "greenpeace.org", or "gopher.epa.gov".

❒ Folk tales: AOL features the American Folktale Project wherein students can write their own stories for others to read and discuss.

❒ Geography: The Internet is a great place to learn about geography and collect maps from around the world. AOL has some really nice resources, including "ABC" , "Library", or "National Geographic".

❒ Government: E-mail the President or various government officials.

❐ Library of Congress: Access a few of the thousands of treasures from the WWW. Enter: http://lcweb.loc.gov/.

❐ Literature: Do you know William Shakespeare has a Web site? The ideas for a Lit teacher are endless. Enter the following address: http://the-tech.mit.edu/Shakespeare/works.html.

❐ Newspaper: Create your own online school newspaper.

❐ Pen-Pals: A long standing favorite can be updated via Internet E-mail. Consider the many other ways to improve the writing process online.

❐ Pets: Do science reports on the pets represented in your class. There are a host of newsgroups about pets.

❐ Polls: Conduct an online poll on the topic of your choice.

❐ Star gaze: Join an astronomy forum. AOL has a nifty one.

❐ Story Starters: Have students begin a story. Share the story beginning with another online classroom for development. Have the story concluded by still other online classrooms.

Innovative Internet Applications

Listed below are numerous applications of Internet technology for teachers and students. They include a broad assortment of applications and innovative ways of utilizing the technology for educational purposes in general.

1. Educational Newsgroups: Log onto the Internet and access your NewsWatcher (or any newsreader) so that you can subscribe to any of the following Newsgroups.

k12.chat. teacher
k12.chat.elementary
k12.chat.junior
k12.chat.senior
k12.ed.special

2. Search Tools: Use one of the many gopher browsing tools to initiate in depth information searches. Many gophers allow you to search not only text based materials, but related picture, sound, and video material as well. With a gopher you can both browse for information as well as download the information to your personal computer. Some gophers will give you access to a host of archival information found on the Archie file. Gophers can also connect you to an assortment of electronic phone books for regions across the United States. Popular gopher client software includes:
-- TurboGopher or TurboGopher VR (for Macs)
-- HGopher, WSGopher, or Chameleon (for Windows)

3. Special Web Pages: If exploring the Web, check out two informative educational arenas:

The K-12 Outpost: http//k12.cnidr.org
Apple's Educator Page: http://www.info.apple.com.education

4. ERIC Online: Many classroom teachers who are advancing their level of certification or who may be part of a graduate school program hail the ERIC database information system. This resource has been around for years, and just keeps getting better and better. The educational database was once available only via university library systems or intermediate school district library systems. It has been a frequently used source for securing educational research articles on large numbers of education related topics. ERIC is now available on many Internet sites.

5. Let's Talk - Education: Live chat is one of the most popular applications of Internet technology to date. Live chat allows you to have online conversations with people around the world. Live chat is easy to access and use. Once on the Internet, you will find a vast array of live chat arenas. You should be aware that there are hundreds of live chat possibilities dedicated to any number of live chat topical themes. I've noted just one that might be of special interest to educators. It is easily accessible and easy to use, but only if you are an America Online subscriber.

* America Online: Log on and opt for an *electronic conference room*. Using the keyword ESH, locate the *Electronic Schoolhouse*. Within the ESH is *the schoolroom*, which is where many teachers hang out. You can engage in live chat in order to talk about issues, concerns, or just to exchange ideas.

* For those non-AOL users, several chat groups are available if you can access Telenet in order to connect with a computer using an IRC client. You made need a little advice from a "techie" for these groups, but, if persistent, you can find a way. Once you've connected to an IRC server, any of the following addresses will get you to a live chat education group.

csz.bu.edu	Massachusetts
irc.colorado.edu.	Colorado
irc.uiuc.edu	Illinois

6. Homework Help: Sometimes the questions that students have are not always going to arise during school hours. Wouldn't it be nice for students to have help available during evening hours when many are *doing* their homework? The Internet to the rescue! There are dozens of bulletin boards, chat rooms, and forums, that give students the opportunity to ask for help with any number of school related homework problems. Many of these services have *real teachers online* to answer student homework questions. Commercial service providers often recruit teachers to become online electronic tutors. Teachers are usually reimbursed for their time with free online time with the service provider. Because these tutors are real professionals, adults can worry less about the students who just want easy answers. Online tutors will work through your students questions, offering tips and explaining procedures - not just doling out answers. Below are listed a few of the places where homework help may be found.

⇧ America Online: Academic Assistance Center. Search word - "homework". Live chat with real teachers between 5:00 pm and 1:00 am every day {EST}. In addition to this service, AOL provides a teacher paging service. Search word - "teacher pager". Type in your grade level, your question, and click send. E-mail answers are guaranteed within 48 hours.

Homework help is also available for university students if your work is research based. Once in the AAC, enter "research".

⇧ Any Internet Source: Teacher paging on the Internet or with any CSP. Enter this address: homework24@aol.com.

⇧ Compuserve: see the Student's Forum. Search word - "go stufo".

⇧ GEnie: Access the Computer Assisted Learning Center. Homework questions are posted by subject. Real time chat is available Mondays and Wednesdays, 9:00 pm - 10:00 pm {EST} & Tuesdays and Thursdays, 10:00 - 11:00 pm {EST}.

⇧ Prodigy: Access the Education Bulletin Board or Homework Helper. Helper is a premium service and an extra charge is assigned for services rendered.

7. Publications: Keep in mind that most commercial service providers have dozens of newspapers and magazines online. A few of these include *National Geographic, Newsweek, New York Times, Time Magazine, and U.S. News.*

Why Students Respond to Learning Online

Educators have before them a multitude of goals and responsibilities. Among the most important of the responsibilities that a teacher may have is allowing each child to rise to their highest individual intellectual potential. In order to accomplish this goal we must examine what kinds of experiences children are having as they interface with our educational system. What are student's general attitudes toward school, specific subjects, and their own self concept? Some studies have indicated that there has been a significant decline in student motivation toward academic achievement as of the early eighties (Eccles, Midgley, & Adler, 1984).

Talk to experienced teachers and they will not find this surprising. Teachers have long maintained that the two biggest challenges facing the profession today are classroom management issues and keeping students motivated to learn. Substantial drops in student motivation, curiosity, and enthusiasm as they relate to school and grade related changes are unsettling. Many teachers share dramatic testimonies of decreased motivation as children leave early elementary classrooms and enter middle school. It seems the older children get the more negative they perceive themselves and the more pessimistic they feel about schooling.

Preschoolers find frequent and immediate success in many of the tasks designed for them. Older primary children have fewer tasks designed to guarantee success, and frequently are subjected to instructional material that they are not ready for. This sets up many children for a failing precedent, spiraling them toward an inevitable state of learned helplessness. Students entering middle school confront major shifts in teaching methodology from earlier grades. The atmosphere for many students becomes competitive. Students may sense they are being addressed in a collective manner that is much less personal than former instructional styles. Likewise, assessment and grading schemes become more structured. How can teachers optimize student motivation in the midst of such realities?

Many educators have discovered that providing students with access to new learning technologies does wonders for classroom motivation. While it is true that motivation is more easily stimulated than maintained, there seems to be little doubt that students in general *love* technology.

Why is it that students seem to have such affection for a medium that many adults find intimidating and confusing? Perhaps one reason lies in the reality that children have grown up with technology. It has always been a part of of their experience. Preschoolers see a computer as an extended TV. It gives them pleasure, entertainment, and information. As children grow older they rely on technology for their music, their games, and as an aid to their studies.

As technology relates to a learner's academic studies, it is interesting to consider a few of the many possible reasons why online learning has become so very appealing.

1. Internet technology may increase the amount of **attention** students direct toward a learning task. Attention is a required condition for motivation simply because learners must attend to instructional elements in order to gain mastery over various instructional goals and objectives. Like motivation, gaining a learner's attention is much easier than sustaining it. Attention span is largely dominated by developmental constraints and teachers quickly realize that in order to sustain attention children must be actively involved in the learning processes. Frustrated by trying to design daily activities that actively engage students in every subject every day, many teachers begin to rely upon paper and pencil activities that occupy students with busy work so that teachers can keep up with the demands of lesson planning, evaluation, and report-making. As easy as it is to criticize what appears to be an "easy way out", dittos and conventional assignments are often used as survival mechanisms for teachers who have too much to do and too little time to do it. Online learning allows teachers to engage their students in active and constructive learning while simultaneously increasing professional opportunities to conference

with their students and evaluate them in meaningful ways.

Furthermore, attention is increased by the number of *sensory modalities* stimulated by Internet access. The presence of text, graphics, pictorial, and audio information presented in simultaneous contexts assist in maintaining student attention.

2. Internet technology may increase the degree to which learners perceive information to be **relevant**. Relevance suggests that learners perceive the content of the material they are interacting with is both substantive and important enough to warrant attention and manipulation. The information age has resulted in a deluge of transitory data and a colossal repository of factual information. Conventional instruction has attempted to integrate such information within a learner's life experience through memorization and recall. Because the amount of information has increased so dramatically in our society, education has tried to play "catch up" by having students process more and more data. Meanwhile, the amount of time spent analyzing, discussing, and exploring the implications of new information in conventional classrooms has received less attention.

Online learning requires students to synthesize data into meaningful and useful applications. TBLPs allow students to exchange novel ideas and indulge in academic exchanges in personalized ways. By so doing, the information becomes useful and relevant as opposed to being sifted through in a maze of contexts which promote academic trivia and objective quizzes. Internet technology can help learners integrate information in more meaningful contexts. It allows learners to search and select data on any given topic. It provides them with opportunities to invest themselves in the pursuit of knowledge, the presentation of knowledge, and an evaluation of the experience as a whole.

3. Online learning increases a student's sense of **competence and control** over learning activities (Rivard, 1995). When students believe that they can perform competently in school, they exhibit high levels of confidence. Learners are motivated when they perceive themselves as successful. Success becomes a predictor for future successes, as confidence breeds increased confidence. Unfortunately, many conventional school assignments have not nurtured confidence or control in students. When learners lose control of their own learning and become directed by others who might undermine student autonomy and confidence, it is reasonable to expect that students will

be unmotivated and troublesome. Online learning becomes a means by which classrooms can be re-structured so that teachers and students are placed in a "win/win" situation. Learners regain varying degrees of control and regulation while teachers are provided with greater instructional opportunities.

4. Online learning increases levels of student **satisfaction** in learning. Learners are satisfied when they have fulfilled a need to achieve. The need to achieve can be based on internal or external elements. Internet TBLPs may be designed so that learners work toward inner satisfaction and are less concerned about the need to achieve based upon social comparisons and teacher expectations. As much as we must orient children to have their own needs met, teachers must work to have their own needs met too. Teachers who bask in the satisfaction that children are "working for them" may need to re-evaluate the context of their professional aspirations. It is far better for students to be working for themselves than it is for them to be working for a teacher. Children often exhibit needs for approval in a variety of ways and degrees. Technology does not usurp the approval children may receive from teachers or peers. It does help to define the locus of satisfaction for a learner however, so that "approval" becomes something of more permanent value.

REFERENCES

Eccles, J., Midgley, C., & Adler, T. (1984). Grade Related Changes in the School Environment: Effects on Achievement Motivation. In J. Nichols {Ed.}, *Advances in Motivation and Achievement.* Vol.3 Greenwich, CT: JAI Press.

Rivard, Joseph. (1995). *Select Topics on Technology, Teaching, & Learning.* Needham Heights, MA: Simon & Schuster.

Part Six: Consider the Future

The following story has been designed as a vehicle to prompt thoughtful reflection about the future of technology in education. As you apply technology based lesson plans in your classrooms, you will quickly observe how rapidly technology advances. As you read, consider this story as a futuristic illustration to think critically about. There are elements in the story that may be interpreted as positive statements regarding the future of technology in education. Other elements in the story may serve as cautionary statements about potential uses and abuses of technology in education. After you have read the story, take a moment and consider the best and worst features of this futuristic classroom. Summarize your reactions and consider responding to the story by sending me a note via Internet e-mail. My address in listed in the opening pages of this Guide.

The Virtual Classroom

A Short Story by
Joseph Rivard

It was 7:00 am when the voice activated alarm awoke thirteen-year-old Chris from a very deep sleep. It was Monday morning and the sound of his mother's voice electronically duplicated by his alarm brought him little comfort as he realized the weekend was over and it was back to school today. Crawling slowly out of bed he slipped on a robe and went downstairs to get some breakfast. With his dad out of town on business and his mom having already gone out for the day, he sleepily consumed his favorite cereal, sipped his orange juice, and read a short note left by his mother. He was bored by the predictability of the script: a list of after-school chores to be done and several options suggested for his dinner. Given some money left on the table and the invitation to eat out with his best friend, he ignored any other possibilities and was gladdened by the thought of having some social time at the end of such a foreboding Monday morning. Chris was hardly enamored with school, and while he had long since resigned himself to its inevitability, he didn't pretend to look forward to the way it drained his emotions and taxed his mind. He always returned so exhausted...

As Chris finished his breakfast he began to feel himself lose the morning "groggies", and knew that a shower would really bring him up to speed. Double stepping the stairs he was quickly back in his room. The clock announced the time quarterly, and Chris realized that somewhere he had lost twenty minutes. The shower had best be a quick one, and as he stepped into the steamy stall he savored the feel of the hot water on his skin. If only he could spend today outdoors. Chris loved the feel of natural elements against his flesh. Wind, rain, sun... it didn't matter. As long as it was real.

Climbing out of the shower, Chris surveyed the condition of his room. A twelve by fourteen state of confusion. The closet door stared gapingly open before him revealing an unprecedented amount of clutter within. With dirty clothes piled high in one corner and magazines scattered recklessly around the floor he sensed it was time to clean things up a bit. This thought was prompted not merely because of some intrinsic sense of responsibility, but because his dad was due home Wednesday. Against the wall on his right stood his ever-faithful entertainment system. Chris remained impressed with it massiveness, especially since he had invested years of birthday money and Christmas requests in the construction of the electronic marvel. Yet there was neither time to clean or be entertained he thought, as he slowly glanced to his left. It was time to begin.

Standing conspicuously against the north wall of the room was a small booth. Hanging coldly above the door of the booth was a school uniform. He often called it his diving suit, as it reminded him of the scuba gear divers wore back around 2010. He finished drying himself, dropping his bath towel carelessly on the floor. Slowly he reached for his uniform. As he stepped into it he could feel the rubbery insulation press clammily against his skin. He hated the sensation. It was like putting on a wet bathing suit after you had dried off. He knew that for the next several hours his body was destined to be confined within this synthetic cocoon. Once online, he knew the uniform would become like a second skin, but for the moment he felt as if every pore was suffocating.

Chris dreaded the preliminaries involved in school engagement. He quickly secured his uniform and began a brief systems check. It was essential that the numerous fiber optic cables embedded within the Lycra suit function without flaw. Likewise, the umbilical cord connecting his uniform to his in-house computing booth must be secured. Having made the necessary connections, Chris was ready to go online. He stepped inside the booth and secured the door. The interior of the booth was rather stark. The small walled environment was embellished with a myriad of small screens, LED indicator lights, cameras, microphones, speakers, sensors, and eyewear. Chris could stand or sit with ease, and the reclining cushioned chair seemed the one luxury the booth contained. Encased in blackness, Chris punched the glowing green button marked school engagement on his right. Chris relaxed as he witnessed the system conduct an additional computerized self check on all systems. Only a moment or two passed before the screen confirmed that Chris was indeed online with all systems fully functioning.

Starville Public Schools required a rather precocious log-on procedure. On a small monitor labeled Starville, the system asked Chris to first enter his student ID code. The code was numeric, so he entered his number using a small digital keypad located below the monitor. A small digital clock now displayed real time flashing slowly on the Starville monitor. Fortunately Chris had logged in on time. He couldn't afford another tardy notice, for his parents had warned him that if he was late for school engagement one more time, he would not be able to play CyberTrek with Eming. Such deprivation would be difficult to take, as Chris had found Eming to be an auspicious competitor in the sport. Locally, most of his friends in the neighborhood seemed to have very predictable playing strategies. International competitors like Eming were savored. Her approach to the game was so unlike his own.

Placing his forehead close against an upholstered brace, Chris sat motionless as a laser passed quickly across his right retina. In addition to a retinal scan, Chris was required to submit a hand imprint upon a touch screen to his left, and speak his name for voice recognition by the Starville security system. Finally with his attendance confirmed, Chris was able to access his school dayplan. Speaking clearly into a small microphone, Chris instructed the system.

"Retrieve Dayplan - October 17, 2077 AM
Starville PS #107 - Instructor : Ms. J. Jenkins
Level 8 Student - Christian Weiss."

Chris soon heard the prerecorded voice of Ms. Jenkins welcoming him to the new day's adventure. The general direction contained within each day plan was hardly surprising to Chris, as he and Ms. Jenkins mapped out his academic direction mutually. While the state mandated various aspects of the level eight curricula, a great deal of what was accomplished was at the discretion of Ms. Jenkins and Chris. Starville was proud of the fact that none of its students failed the basic competence required by exiting assessments, and Chris knew that the basic level eight academic skills were hardly challenging. What worried Chris was not the exit exams for level eight. What worried Chris was whether or not he was prepared to handle the problem solving simulations developed by the Starville Life Skills System. Life skills simulations were designed to assess problem solving abilities, and students were individually evaluated for competency in that area. While Chris had selected various areas of academic interest and extra curricular enrichment, he never knew how Ms. Jenkins and the SLS system would use those topics as a vehicle to teach problem solving and life skills.

Glancing at the dayplan, the suspicion that Chris had was confirmed. There were no skills-based lessons offered this morning, and the system informed him that he had the option to engage in a SLS system enactment given one of the following broad contexts.

(1) History - Events leading to World War III
(2) Science - Research History: The Cancer Cure
(3) Art History - 1990-2000
(4) Enrichment - Terrestrial Vehicles/ Early Porsche Sport Automobiles

Chris knew all too well that the options before him were optional only in sequence. What he did not select first would unavoidably return on a future menu to haunt him later in the day or sometime in the future on another dayplan. Nevertheless, Chris was not one to put off pleasure, so he opted for enrichment. He had often shared his passion for terrestrial transportation with Ms. Jenkins, especially his affinity for Porsche sporting land vehicles popular between 1950-1999. Having selected item four, an extensive menu regarding vehicle selection succeeded. Chris was able to select a car of choice {make, model, year}, various automotive options, and even his favorite color. Chris opted for a black 1979 Porsche 928S. Selecting choices from the menu was simple enough, but Chris realized that the core experiences the SLS system would contrive for him would be much more complex. Using information previously programmed by

Ms. Jenkins and SLS consultants he suspected that the life skills adventure ahead of him would hardly be so elementary.

The Starville monitor briefly marked real time once again before a viewing field was lowered from the top of the booth over his head. It was black and silent. Suddenly there appeared a door. He knew that beyond the door was an alternate reality. A reality contrived by SLS. A reality conjured up by information sources outside himself, and responsive to whatever words and actions he would initiate from this point forward. He hesitated before opening the door, realizing that once he stepped into the virtual field he was committed to the conclusion of the exercise. He would be immersed within a world outside of real time and space. With his heart pounding and his muscles tightening he reached for the door.

Weeks earlier Ms. Jenkins had met with SLS technician programmers often referred to as "RC's". RC's were "reality creators", and it was an RC's task to work with professional educators in creating life experiences in an alternate reality. The realities created by the RC's were diverse in nature. The desired outcomes from each experience varied, as there were reality experiences for each of the major academic disciplines per student level. There were also thematic realities which coalesced a number of disciplines in order to perpetuate an interdisciplinary educational approach. There were realities for the arts, and realities for sports and physical fitness. Each of these realities allowed for technical modification by those at SLS, as well as individual student interactivity. The core paths within each primary reality construct were preauthored and distributed by satellite by the National Education Institute. Starville received transmissions at will from this education utility as did thousands of other localized educational sectors.

While the RC's loved to modify the base realities conjured by NEI, there was no greater pleasure for them than the opportunity to fashion individual student enrichment realities. Local RC's had complete autonomy and freedom of design in the creation of the enrichment realities. They worked only with the student's teacher, but were required by law to be licensed for reality creation.

Ms. Jenkins was concise and explicit in the description of what she had in mind. She wanted to provide student Christian Weiss with a life experience exploring the dangers of substance abuse. She was aware of Christian's affinity for 1900's terrestrial sports cars, and believed that a scenario involving drinking and driving might be an effective way to present the dangers involved in the digestion of unauthorized chemical substances. The reality should depict an accurate rendering of the implications of drinking and driving as it would relate to whatever context Chris might select.

Obtaining information regarding the various makes and models of the Porsche was easily accomplished by accessing one of several automotive hobby databases. Hundreds of minute details for each model were fed into the SLS system. Regardless of the Porsche that Chris might select, SLS could translate the information into a virtual vehicle capable of being virtually driven down any number of roads and highways defined by script. Ms. Jenkins had determined that she would invite Mr. and Mrs. Weiss to meet Chris within the reality as a part of the life experience. The experience would begin with a birthday party at Christian's house celebrating his sixteenth birthday. His mom and dad would then take him out to the garage and hand him a set of keys. Upon opening the garage door Chris would find the Porsche of his dreams. Present would also be Christian's best friend. Together they would be encouraged to take the car out for a drive. Christian's best friend would be a virtual construction however, preprogrammed to initiate a series of events within the reality. Among other things, he would encourage Chris to pick up some alcohol so that they could really celebrate the occasion of his birthday.

There were any number of choices Chris could make throughout the experience, but the SLS technicians were reasonably certain that the combined enticements of both speed and alcohol would cooperate to create at least one "worse case" scenario. Given the geographic parameters of the script it was likely that if all the *wrong* choices were made, Chris would end up south bound on Michigan Interstate 75 at the M59 west exit ramp. There, Chris and his best friend would lose control of the vehicle being driven as they were trying to maneuver a sharp curve rising abruptly from the exit ramp. Of course that was a worse case scenario. With each RC having a bit of Hollywood within, they looked forward to creating a number of different dramas capable of occurring depending upon the choices Chris would make within his virtual life experience.

It was a perfect night. Chris couldn't believe he was actually at the wheel of this ebony angel. The 4664 cc engine sang as it cut through the night. The stereo pumped energy into the cockpit as his best friend urged Chris to open it up a bit as they cruised the last few miles of the expressway before reaching home. Chris punched the accelerator and could feel the strength of 300bhp pushing him back into the leather bucket. The 928's 0.38 drag coefficient allowed the phantom to slice through the darkness as Chris glanced at the speedometer. Eighty five, ninety, one hundred miles an hour. What a car! Strong and stable, there was little to prove their speed nary the speedometer and the rate at which the highway lampposts disappeared in succession.

Chris was driven by the speed, and fueled by a subtle arrogance from the few drinks he had consumed earlier. He was enjoying just a slight buzz. A bit light headed, happy, and confident, Chris pursued the challenge prompted by his friend. Faster...faster. One hundred and ten, one hundred and twenty, one hundred and thirty. Chris could feel every sensation, every vibration. Every sound made him feel so alive, every image pressed brilliantly in his memory. He was excited, enticed, and enamored. Still he was twenty five mph short of the 928's capable top speed. Chris pulled his foot from the accelerator, deciding to save something for the next time out. As he did so he realized he was nearly on top of the M59 exit ramp. Chris braked hard and heard rubber tearing from the concrete. His heart was pounding, his blood pressure rising. The 928 never made the curve. It was a one hundred and five mile an hour projectile hurtling over the embankment. Chris could feel himself floating in mid air. It was if he were moving in slow motion. He looked to his right and saw the terror across his friend's face. He heard the scream of shearing metal and the shatter of glass. He felt the crash and experienced some tremendous pressure against his chest. He heard his friend scream as he realized the car roof was caving in. Terror consumed him as darkness tore the light from his eyes and engulfed him.

The SLS technicians monitored Christian's heartbeat and blood pressure carefully. It was silent within the booth now, with only the heavy breathing of the displaced thirteen year old audible to the RC's. They were quite pleased. The reality they had contrived for Chris worked flawlessly. It was standard operating procedure to allow the subject some quiet time prior to establishing real time audio or visual communication. Chris would need a little orientation time prior to completing the debriefing which succeeded each life skills experience. It was Chris who initiated real time communication first. He was reporting VIM sickness. Visually induced motion sickness was common for reality experiences such as the one Chris had just completed. Immersed within his three dimensional reality, Chris was exposed to numerous visual, aural, and haptic cues during his experience. However the absence of movement cues from within his body caused him to become disoriented.

Chris made it out of the booth and into the bathroom just in time. The nausea was overwhelming and his favorite morning cereal reappeared in the midday vomit. It was now lunchtime, but he had little desire to try to eat again. He could join some of his friends in one of their favorite virtual games, but for the moment seemed simply content to lay and rest. He opened his bedroom window and felt a cool breeze sweep softly against his skin. Back in real time... it felt good. Suddenly he felt the need to see his best friend. His death seemed so authentic. Memories flooded his mind as the life experience recreated itself in his thoughts. Interrupted by his beeping pager, Chris realized it was time to re-engage. As he walked wearily toward the booth he wondered what Ms. Jenkins had in store for him this afternoon.

Part Seven: Your Address Book

World Wide Web Resources for Educators

Title: A.Word.A Day
Description: Vocabulary development
Address: **http://1rdc5.1rdc.pitt.edu/awad/home.html**

Title: Academy One
Description: K-12 Internet projects
Address: **http://www.nptn.org:80/cyber.serv/AOneP/**

Title: Adult Education
Description: Adult Education
Address: **http://galaxy.einet.net/galaxy/Social-Sciences/Education/Adult-Education.html**

Title: American Educational Research Association
Description: Professional association
Address: **http://tikkun.ed.asu.edu/aera/home.html**

Title: AIMS Educational Foundation
Description: K-9 Math & Science
Address: **http://204.161.33.100/AIMS.html**

Title: Ainsworth Keyboard Training
Description: Keyboard skill training
Address: **http://www.qwerty.com**

Title: Allyn & Bacon
Description: Education resources
Address: **http://www.abacon.com**

Title: American Assoc. of Core Curriculum
Description: Curriculum resources
Address: **gopher://mercury.cair.du.edu:70/11/gophers/public_policy/**

Title: Ameritech Education Resources
Description: Lesson plans, curriculum guides, projects
Address: **http://www.aads.net:1081/education/**

Title: Amistad Research Center
Description: African American history & culture
Address: **http://www.arc.tulane.edu/**

Title: Apple Virtual Campus
Description: Innovative uses of new technologies
Address: **http://www.info.apple.com/hed/**

Title: Aristotle
Description: Online newspaper
Address: **http://aristotle.isu.edu**

Title: Arizona State University
Description: Ed resources, grants, and product information
Address: **gopher://info.asu.edu/11/asu-cwis/education/other**

Title: Arkansas K-12 Gopher
Description: Education news, workshops, references
Address: **gopher://hp.k12.ar.us**

Title: Armadillo's WWW Server
Description: Texas history and culture
Address: **http://chico.rice.edu/armadillo**

Title: Arrow Publishing
Description: Literacy materials
Address: **http://www2.interpath.net:80/spadion/arrow/**

Title: ArtsEdge
Description: K-12 art resources
Address: **http://artsedge.kennedy-center.org/artsedge.html**

Title: AskERIC
Description: ERIC documents
Address: **http://ericir.syr.edu**

Title: Banned Books Online
Description: Censorship issues
Address: **http://www.cs.cmu.edu:8001/
Web/People/spok/banned-books.html**

Title: Biology
Description: K-12 Science
Address: **http://galaxy.einet.net/galaxy/Science/Biology.html**

Title: Book Nook
Description: Book reports by children
Address: **http://i-site.on.ca/Isite/Education/Bk_report/**

Title: Busy Teachers Web Site
Description: K-12 Internet resources
Address: **http://www.gatech.edu/1cc/idt/Students/Cole/proj/K-12/TOC.html**

Title: Canadian Kids' Page
Description: Kid stuff
Address: **http://www.onramp.ca/~lowens/107kids.htm**

Title: Carrie's Sites
Description: Education resources
Address: **http://www.mtjeff.com/~bodenst/page5.html**

Title: Cartoon Laws of Physics
Description: Physics cartoons
Address: **http://abacus.bates.edu/~jburke/open1/physics.html**

Title: CASAA
Description: Student leadership materials
Address: **http://www.sentex.net/~casaa**

Title: CTY
Description: Resources for gifted students
Address: **http://www.jhu.edu:80/~gifted/**

Title: CEPS/NASM
Description: Astronomy and planetary information
Address: **http://ceps.nasm.edu:2020/homepage.html**

Title: Childaware
Description: Preschool information & resources
Address: **http://www.inetcom.net/test/index.html**

Title: Children's Literature
Description: Books, author information, online publications
Address: **http://www.ucalgary.ca/~dkbrown/index.html**

Title: Cisco Education Resources
Description: School networking projects
Address: **http://sunsite.unc.edu/cisco/edu-arch.html**

Title: Classroom at the Internet Schoolhouse
Description: Internet projects, art, games, ideas
Address: **http://www.packet.net:80/schoolhouse/inside.html**

Title: Classroom Connect
Description: Online magazine
Address: **http://www.wentworth.com/classroom**

Title: CNN
Description: Newservice
Address: **gopher://ericir.syr.edu:70/11/Lesson/CNN**

Title: Computer as Learning Partner
Description: Middle School Science
Address: **http://www.clp.berkely.edu/CLP.html**

Title: CyberKids Home
Description: Kids resources
Address: **http://www.woodwind.com:80/cyberkids/**

Title: Cyberspace Middle School
Description: Links to online middle school resources
Address: **http://www.ascri.fsu.edu/~dennisl/CMS.html**

Title: Digital Frog
Description: CD-ROM, educational software
Address: **http://www.sentex.net/~dfi**

Title: Digital Tradition
Description: Children's songs
Address: **http://web2.xerox.com/digitrad/**

Title: Dole 5
Description: Nutrition information
Address: **http://www.dole5aday.com**

Title: Eagle Ridge
Description: Native America, wildlife, environmental info
Address: **http://www.primenet.com/~eaglerg/**

Title: Education
Description: Social Sciences
Address: **http://aw.com/educatio.html**

Title: Education Sites
Description: Internet subject guide to sources
Address: **http://www.fn.net/education.html**

Title: Education Virtual Library
Description: Foreign language resources
Address: **http://www.csu.edu.au/education/primary.html**

Title: Educational Software Institute
Description: 19 categories of K-12 software
Address: **http://www.bonsai.com/q/edsoftcat/htdocs/esihome.html**

Title: eduMall
Description: Education product information
Address: **http://edumall.com/**

Title: Egyptian Gallery
Description: Ancient and contemporary Egypt
Address: **http://www.mordor.com/hany/egypt/egypt.html**

Title: Electronic Prehistoric Shark Museum
Description: Sharks
Address: **http://turnpike.net/emporium/C/celestial/epsm.htm**

Title: ESL
Description: English as a second language
Address: **http://www.ed.uiuc.edu/edpsy-387/rongchang-li/esl/**

Title: Environmental Education Network
Description: Environmental issues
Address: **http://www.envirolink.org/enviroed/**

Title: ESU #16 Gopher
Description: Nebraska's K-12 education network
Address: **gopher://esu16.esu16.k12.ne.us**

Title: eWorld on the Web
Description: Electronic learning community
Address: **http://www.eworld.com/education/resources**

Title: Explorer Home Page
Description: Math & Science curriculum resources
Address: **http://server2.greatlakes.k12.mi.us/**

Title: Friends & Partners
Description: U.S./Russian cultural connection
Address: **http://solar.rtd.utk.edu/friends/home.html**

Title: Galileo
Description: K-12 Science
Address: **http://wwwhpcc.astro.washington.edu/scied/galileo.html**

Title: GCRIO
Description: Interactive science projects
Address: **http://www.gcrio.org/eduStd.html**

Title: GENII Home Page
Description: Internet resources for teachers
Address: **http://www.deakin.edu.au/edu/MSEE/GENII/GENII-Home-Page.html**

Title: Geometry Forum
Description: Math
Address: **http://forum.swarthmore.edu/**

Title: Gifted & Talented
Description: Gifted and talented resources
Address: **http://www.eskimo.com:80/~user/kids.html**

Title: Grolier Interactive
Description: Online encyclopedia
Address: **http://www.grolier.com**

Title: Hello India!
Description: Indian food, music, culture
Address: **http://www.helloindia.com**

Title: Heritage Map Museum
Description: Historic maps
Address: **http://www.carto.com**

Title: Holocaust
Description: Holocaust resource materials
Address: **gopher://info.asu.edu:70/11/asu-cwis/education/other/k12resources/holocaust**

Title: Homework Page
Description: Homework help
Address: **http://www.tpoint.net/~jewels/homework.html**

Title: Inkspot
Description: Young writers information
Address: **http://www.interlog.com/~ohi/dmo-pages/young.html**

Title: Interactive Frog Dissection
Description: Science
Address: **http://curry.edschool.Virginia.edu:80/~insttech/frog/**

Title: ISN KidNews
Description: News service for kids
Address: **http://www.umassd.edu/SpecialPrograms/ISN/KidNews.html**

Title: Kids' Space
Description: Applied computer skills
Address: **http://www.interport.net/~sachi**

Title: Live from Antarctica
Description: Field journals & question and answers
Address: **http://quest.arc.nasa.gov/livefrom/livefrom.html**

Title: Mark Twain Library
Description: Collected works
Address: **http://hydor.colorado.edu/twain/**

Title: Math Education Resources
Description: Plans, guides, links
Address: **http://www.teleport.com/~vincer/math.html**

Title: Minnesota Center for Arts
Description: Art education
Address: **gopher://gopher.mcae.k12.mn.us:70/1**

Title: Mount St. Helens
Description: Volcano - pictures and information
Address: **http://volcano.und.nodak.edu/vdocs/msh/msh/html**

Title: NASA Education
Description: Space science
Address: **http://quest.arc.nasa.gov,http://k12mac.larc.nasa.gov**

Title: Network Nuggets
Description: Daily messages regarding new Internet resources
Address: **http://www.etc.bc.ca/~tcoop/index.html**

Title: Newton's Apple
Description: Plans from the TV show
Address: **http://ericir.syr.edu/Newton/welcome.html**

Title: Nine Planets
Description: Multimedia solar system
Address: **http://seds.lpl.arizona.edu/nineplanets/nineplanets/nineplanets.html#to**

Title: ICICLE
Description: K-12 curriculum & instruction materials
Address: **http://calvin.cc.ndsu.nodak.edu/wayne/icicle.html**

Title: Online Books
Description: Books
Address: **http://www.cs.cmu.edu:8001/Web/books.html**

Title: PBS K-12 Learning
Description: Instructional television resources
Address: **http://mumford.pbs.org/learning/k12/**

Title: Weather Pages
Description: Weather information & statistics
Address: **http://www.ems.psu.edu/wx/**

Title: Project LEAP
Description: Family & workplace literacy, job skills, GED
Address: **http://www.olemiss.edu/depts/project_leap**

Title: Reading & Language Arts Library
Description: Books, author info, portfolio assessments
Address: **gopher://scholastic.com:2003/11/**

Title: Schoolhouse Videos & CDs
Description: Videos and CDs - diverse topics
Address: **http://www.nando.net/ads/gift/school.htm**

Title: Teacher Talk
Description: Discussion & resources
Address: **http://www.mightymedia.com/talk/working.hmt**

Title: Technology, Teaching, & Learning
Description: Curricular resource for K-12 technology integration, restructuring with technology
Address: **http://www.ehhs.cmich.edu/~rlamb/tech.teach.learn.html**

Title: UEWeb
Description: Focus on urban education
Address: **http://eric-web.tc.columbia.edu/**

Title: Videodiscovery
Description: CD-ROM & laser disc resources
Address: **http://www.videodiscovery.com/vdyweb**

Title: Violence.prev
Description: Violence prevention programs & information
Address: **gopher://gopher.edu.gov.on.ca:70/11/english/schools/violence.prev**

Title: Welcome to the Civil War Center
Description: Civil War materials and resources
Address: **http://www.cwc.lsu.edu/**

Title: Whales
Description: Grade K-5 thematic unit
Address: **http://curry.edschool.Virginia.EDU/~kpj5e/Whales/Contents.HTML**

Title: World Kids
Description: PK-3rd foreign language information
Address: **http://www.webpup.com/worldkids/**

Title: World Lecture Hall
Description: Notes & plans on diverse subjects
Address: **http://www.utexas.edu/world/lecture/**

Title: World of Benjamin Franklin
Description: Multimedia information about Ben Franklin
Address: **http://sln.fi.edu/franklin/rotten.html**

Title: World of Vikings
Description: CD-ROM resources on Vikings
Address: **http://www.demon.co.uk/history/vikings/vikhome.html**

Title: Writing at MU
Description: Discussion site for writers
Address: **http://www.missouri.edu/~wleric/writery.html**

NOTES

Use this space to add additional addresses as you explore the WWW...

Title:
Description:
Address:

Title:
Description:
Address:

Title:
Description:
Address:

Title:
Description:
Address:

Title:
Description:
Address:

Title:
Description:
Address:

Title:
Description:
Address:

NOTES

Use this space to add additional addresses as you explore the WWW...

Title:
Description:
Address:

Title:
Description:
Address:

Title:
Description:
Address:

Title:
Description:
Address:

Title:
Description:
Address:

Title:
Description:
Address:

Title:
Description:
Address:

NOTES

Use this space to add additional addresses as you explore the WWW...

Title:
Description:
Address:

Title:
Description:
Address:

Title:
Description:
Address:

Title:
Description:
Address:

Title:
Description:
Address:

Title:
Description:
Address:

Title:
Description:
Address:

INDEX

Additional Books By the Author

Technology, Teaching, and Learning
Simon & Schuster
ISBN 0-536-58901-1
1-800-374-1200

Technology, Teaching, and Learning is a comprehensive volume addressing the many issues educators face as they attempt to integrate technology within K-12 and higher education curricula.

The Author Online

Internet E-Mail at: 34c5ous @ cmuvm.csv.cmich.edu
Web Page :http://www.ehhs.cmich.edu/rlamb/tech.teach.learn.html
or write
Joseph D. Rivard Ph.D.
Central Michigan University
TEPD-Ronan Hall
Mt. Pleasant, MI 48859